Kaitlynne
Thank you
a copy of
and it means a lot to be able to
share it with people.
Bryson Bolanatz

L.O.V.E

♡

Copyright © 2019 by B.T. Bolianatz

All rights reserved. No part of this publication may be reproduced, distributed, or transmitted in any form or by any means, including photocopying, recording, or other electronic or mechanical methods, without the prior written permission of the publisher, except in the case of brief quotations embodied in critical reviews and certain other noncommercial uses permitted by copyright law.

We will all lose ourselves in something. Enjoy the freedom. You were made for it.

Dear Reader...

I've tossed and turned about how I want to start this book. I had two introductions previously written, but I didn't think either of them were adequate enough to introduce you to what you are about to read. They seemed too forced, and I realized that the last thing I wanted to do was pretend to be somebody I'm not right at the beginning of my most ambitious project to date. Y'see, it's like this: the entire nature of this short volume is meant to be an authentic experience into what I think life is about. And one of the main things that I dislike nowadays is that everyone tries to be somebody they aren't. So, I deleted the last two introductions, and here I am, starting fresh again. Because the truth is, whenever I think of poetry, I always tend to think of all the greats; these men and women who were shrouded in mystery because of what they wrote. A part of me thinks that it would be cool to forge this identity for myself. A great literary writer who people struggle to understand but simultaneously look up to. But to be completely honest, I know that isn't me. I'm not a literary genius (at least not a self-proclaimed genius, anyway), and I don't want to be someone who people struggle to understand. What I am is a life enthusiast. I've always enjoyed writing, but up until this point, I have written fiction; thriller short stories. And while I enjoy writing these stories, I realized not long ago that my true zest for life comes from just discussing life itself. And I didn't really think that there would be a way to discuss the things I enjoy and wonder about in life while still exercising my talent and love for writing. Until I found poetry.

The other thing that I am (as well as a life enthusiast) is a songwriter. I write songs with my brother so that we can play them in my band. My songs are always a release for me, because I can talk about whatever I want. But when I discovered the beauty behind poetry, I realized that the whole concept was basically just writing songs without music. Only in this case, it's a lot less constricting, because I don't have to worry about matching music to my words or coming up with a clever rhyme scheme. I can just write.

The name of this short volume is L.O.V.E.

L.O.V.E. stands for

Lose

Ourselves

Very (quickly in)

Everything

I first thought of the acronym for the title when I was in the shower. I think a lot when I'm in the shower; a lot of these poems have been birthed when I was washing my hair. When it first came into my head, I realized that it was actually the perfect way to describe what love is. I think sometimes, as human beings, we become so focused and so obsessed with loving something or someone that one day we wake up and realize that we have actually let ourselves become lost in this love. Sometimes, that's a good thing. Other times, not so much.

But the point of this is to not let yourself get lost. Rather, these poems were written so that everyone could witness firsthand what I love about life and how I approach living, and that sometimes, maybe getting lost will help you love more ferociously than ever before.

In that way, I believe this book embodies everything that it takes to be a human being. There is a part of me in every one of these poems. When I first started writing this, I can remember being on the phone with the drummer of my band and saying:

"Y'know man, I just want to make something REAL, y'know what I mean? In this day and age there's so much shit going on in the world, and I just want to write something pure and good and real. Something that will spark actual, legitimate conversation. A no bullshit account on what it's like to be a human being. A book that will make people feel deeply about their lives."

And I don't think I'll ever forget his reply, because it was the assurance that I needed to finish the book you are now holding. He said:

"Yeah man. Isn't that what all that literature stuff is supposed to do anyway? Send your message out, my friend."

And so I did. This is my message. And I couldn't be happier with it. Because this is me, in a book. A piece of me and my love and zest and enthusiasm will forever be engrained in these pages, and that's what I think is important. If a piece of me is always around, it means that people can always turn to me if they need help, laughter, or assurance.

I should also probably tell you that because I wanted this experience to be an authentic look into the human mind, the editing to these poems was minimal.

Obviously I checked for spelling errors and basic sentence structure that kind of thing, but the *content* itself, the actual body of the poems, were left mostly untouched. It's not that I was trying to be sloppy with my diction or content choice. I just think that if I can put words on paper EXACTLY how I thought them, other people might be able to relate on a deeper level. Again, no sugar coating or bullshit. These things came straight from my mind onto the page, and I feel like I wouldn't be able to call it authentic had I made meaningless changes to poems that are essentially just thought impulses.

Because I think that's how the human mind works. Sometimes we say things or do things that may have turned out better if we would have gone about them in a different way, but we can't go back and change them. I knew from the start that if I wanted this book to be an accurate depiction of the human experience, I had to let things come naturally, just as I thought them.

And so, what you hold in your hands is the result my efforts. I hope you can find the same kind of solace that I found in these pages. Like it says on the front, these are poems to live to, smile to, sleep to, and laugh to. This is a book you can fall asleep reading, drop in the bathtub, and use as a coaster for your whiskey or wine. You can crinkle the cover, dog-ear the pages, and circle your favorite lines. I give you permission to do all this with my book, and more if you like.

So long as you remember that we are all human, trying to get through life by doing what we love with who we love.

Hell, as long as you remember to wake up every day and love *something*, that's good enough for me.

Enjoy, my friends.

Bryson Tyrick Bolianatz

I hope I don't end up deleting that introduction. It was the best one yet, I think.

This one is for both my grandmas,

Phyllis and Joyce.

Kitchens

I want to be the boy who

Dances in the kitchen to our favorite records

Elton John

Sinatra

And when supper is done, the dancing shoes come

Off

But the music will stay

On

Flakes

What if our troubles are like snowflakes? At first, the weather is cold, and there are more than we can count. But just wait, because much like the weather warms and melts the snow

Our troubles will eventually melt.

And pass like running water

Down the street, past the gum wrappers and old baseball cards

Into the sewer grate.

Then the weather will warm, and you'll wonder why you let the snow bother you

In the first place…

Hotel, Motel

Get out, he said. Get out and don't worry. Because life will be life, and things will happen, and you won't get to see them if you don't get out.

So stop expecting a five star hotel

The real adventures happen at the broken **down**, rusted **up**, middle of nowhere side of the road motels.

With wallflowers that you can hardly see

And a neon sign that reads

"WE HAVE COLOR T.V."

A fridge full of ice and a little spilt whiskey

These are the places that you want to be

Get Out of the Bathtub, Marley

Get out of the bathtub, Marley. Before the bubbles surround you and don't let you go. They will suffocate you.

"Will they really do that?" she asks, as she sips wine from the bottle.

No, they won't. But your thoughts will.

So get out of the bathtub, Marley. There are towels on the rack.

7. (Seven)

"I once read that when we die, our brains have seven minutes of activity left, in which our whole lives replay before our eyes. Do you think that will happen to you? I mean, Every moment. In perfect detail. Can you imagine?"

Then your eyes close.

AND IT STARTS.

LADIES AND GENTLEMEN, WELCOME TO THE LIFE OF (INSERT NAME HERE)

It all comes back

The shirt your mother was wearing the night she went into labor.

The feeling of your father's rough, calloused hands the first time he held you.

Your first birthday, then your second. Then your third,

Your fourth, your fifth.

Your first day of kindergarten. Then your last.

First summer vacation. First last day of summer vacation.

Your first night away from home, first loonie you found on the ground, first day in organized sport, and the first time you received a participation medal.

The first time you said a swear word.

Shit.

Damn.

Then the taste of the soap in your mouth.

Shit again. But not out loud this time.

Your first day of high school.

Your first date

The first time you realized your first kiss doesn't always happen on the first date.

Your second date.

First kiss, for real this time.

Your first girlfriend, first time making love, first best friend, first win and first defeat. First drive in a car, first time at the bar, and your first time in a fight.

First (and only) time getting married.

First house. First child. First second child. First try at a third.

First child away at college.

First grey hair.

First mole. First time using a cane.

First day at a nursing home.

First day in fifty years without your wife. She got sick and didn't get better.

First time playing shuffleboard with Bob from room 312.

First time trying a special brownie at age 85. Damn you Bob.

First birthday in the nursing home. First without your wife, too. But your kids came.

First heart attack.

First ride in an ambulance.

First time in the ICU. Bob and the kids came to visit.

One night, after a long day, Bob leans over and says:

"I once read that when we die, our brains have seven minutes of activity left, in which our whole lives replay before our eyes. Do you think that will happen to you? I mean, Every moment. In perfect detail. Can you imagine?"

Then your eyes close.

AND IT STARTS.

LADIES AND GENTLEMEN, WELCOME TO THE LIFE OF (INSERT NAME HERE)

It all comes back

The shirt your mother was wearing the night she went into labor............

Microwave

I think deep down we would all rather spend our nights eating microwave meals

Falling asleep in our clothes

On Grandma's old sofa bed

Next to someone we love.

So let's hope we live long enough

To see ourselves

Hit the stop button on the microwave.

Because the Kraft Dinner won't wait forever

And neither will you

Yellow Pages

Someday I'll wonder why

I still remember

Her number

Without the yellow pages

306-949-50**

I won't write it all

That's what the yellow pages are for.

Give myself a challenge.

Just in case.

$100

"Dad, where did you get this couch?"

Goodwill

"How much did it cost?"

$100

"But it has holes"

Of course it does

"What?"

Someday son, you'll get your heart broken. Then you'll have holes too. And you'll be just like this couch, lonely and alone, hoping that someone will pick you up and take you home.

"Will I have coins in my pockets?"

What?

"The couch dad. I found a coin in the cushion"

That's because something beautiful can always come from something broken. You wouldn't have found that coin without the holes in the cushions

Videos of Home

That song on the scratchy

Lo-fi

Community radio station

Is sometimes enough

To make you feel as though

You are a tourist in your own city

Prompting actions like

Extending your phone Out the window

To take videos of buildings

That you have seen countless times before

But are somehow just seeing for the first time

And as the song plays

You realize

That home is not necessarily the city you are driving through

But rather

The people in the car

Singing songs with you

Orange

There is a box around everyone's heart.

A box that protects us

And when we are lucky, A box that opens…

Every so often so that life seeps in.

But my box is always open.

I find myself consistently thinking about my bedroom, and the walls around it

the walls that I painted orange

And I like to think that those orange walls represent

Everything that I want to be

Bright and vibrant

In a world of greys and browns

And I know a day will come

When I will need to leave the orange walls behind

But I'm not disappointed, because I know

That if I could see the color of the
        box around my heart
    Those walls would be orange too

FRIENDS

F·R·I·E·N·D·S.

Were they ever

True

Friends?

Or was

F·R·I·E·N·D·S

Just made

So that people with no

Friends

Could watch

F·R·I·E·N·D·S

As a type of motivation

To make real

Friends?

WMCTVNR

Have you seen the T.V. lately?

I've been watching it on the daily.

And between puffs of my cigarette

I suppose I had to wonder

Why you insisted the news be on

3 times.

Once in the morning

Once at noon

And once to end off the day.

I mean,

how much sad shit do you need, anyway?

Idealistic Life:

The Beginning to the End in Ten Words

We are born. We live vivaciously. We love. We rest.

UHaul

And when you move in

Promise that you'll hang art

On all four walls

And the roof

Like taking pieces of another world

To make your new one feel more complete

Words

Sometimes

Words just won't do it,

And that's okay.

Sometimes

To understand what you read

You first need to

Write

So go

Live

And write your story

With the things you do

Rather than

The words you write

Drawing of a Breath

The day you realize

You are breathing the same air

You have breathed

Since the day you were born

Is the day you realize

How simple life really is

Regret

And when I am old

My biggest regret will not be the things that I have done

But instead will be

The fact that I neglected to do some of the things

Which make life worth living.

So I will not conform

If conformity comes at the price of my happiness

A Letter to all Those Who Need to Hear it

A Free Verse Poem

Dear [INSERT NAME HERE],

Nowadays, I think people feel as though there is no freedom. The reason I think this is simple: everyone seems to live their life in the exact same way, every single day. They wake up, and immediately they start to consider everything in the coming day that is unenjoyable. I am here to tell you that this is simply not true.

If there was ever a reason to change the way that you live, let it be this letter. Even if you must pretend it's coming from a friend or a lover, heed these words:

You are in control of what happens in your life. And although this may seem like a simple sentence, I know that it isn't. If it were, nobody would be living in the routine that I just discussed. If people really believed they were in control of their own lives, they wouldn't be unhappy. So believe me when you read those words, and take back control of your life.

If you don't like your job, quit.

If money is the issue, find a way to make money doing what you love.

If the people around you are bringing you down, know that only **you** have control over how you feel, and you can choose to sail your ship with positivity.

Although these may seem like lofty requests, they are possible. And if I were you, and one of the above things pertained to me, I would be more scared of continuing to live in unhappiness than I would be to make a change. Consider this:

Have you ever had a day where you wake up, and immediately you feel off? You can just feel in your mind that the day is going to be bad.

And usually, if your day starts like this, it **is** bad. You stumble through the day, and it seems like nothing can go your way.

This is not a coincidence.

The truth of this situation is, the universe gives you what you think about. If you constantly think about what you want, the universe will deliver.

When this idea is applied to the situation I just described, the reason why your day is bad becomes easy to see. You think your day will be bad, so it is.

Although this may seem upsetting to some, that is not the point. If the universe gives you what you think about, it is theoretically just as easy to have a good day as it is to have a bad one.

If you want to have a good day, you just need to truly believe that the coming day will be good. If you want to find success in doing what you love, you must visualize where you want your passion to take you and hold onto it.

If you've gotten to this point in the letter and are still believing what you read, I applaud you. Half the battle of achieving this level of contentedness comes from believing that you can.

And if you've gotten to this point and are skeptical, don't be disheartened. Misunderstanding is not the same as unintelligent. In fact, I don't believe that the word unintelligent should even exist. Just because you know something that another does not doesn't mean that you are unintelligent. All this means is that you specialize in a certain area that someone else has not yet come across.

Think about it like this:

If you put an Olympic swimmer on the edge of a pool beside a person who does not yet know how to swim, of course the Olympic swimmer will win in a race. Does this mean that the other person is in any way less intelligent than the Olympic swimmer? Absolutely not. Because if the non-swimmer was given years of swimming lessons and was conditioned in the exact same way as the Olympic swimmer, the race would be more of a contest when they met.

Just because the non-swimmer was initially unversed in the concept of Olympic swimming, it doesn't mean that he was less intelligent than the Olympian. Because when given time, he was able to reach the same level.

There is no such thing as unintelligent. There is a difference between unintelligent and unknowledgeable. I believe that everyone, in one area or another, is unknowledgeable. School shouldn't measure intelligence. Because given time and resources, everyone can reach the same level of intelligence.

So if you sit in a classroom and get told that have a mere 45 minutes to complete an exam and you then fail said exam, it doesn't mean you are stupid. Because if you would have learned one of the facts on the exam 30 seconds before stepping into the classroom, by their standards, you'd be more intelligent.

See what I mean? Intelligence is nothing. The ability to practice and condition yourself is the true measure of knowledge.

So if you find yourself becoming confused with the concepts of positive thinking that I just discussed, do not stop reading.

Use this letter as conditioning. Read and re read and re read again until you find yourself able to access certain parts of your subconscious that let you manifest your dreams. Don't think of this as something that only the elite can achieve. You have the power to live the best day of your life

EVERY

SINGLE

DAY

And if you don't believe me, my only wish is that you will practice. Practice positivity. Exercise your mind so that it becomes easy to think positively about every aspect of life.

It took me a while. I had to severely change the way I think about certain things in order to get to this new level of happiness. But I did, and look what happened.

The book you are holding is the very result of my efforts. You are literally holding a piece of my positivity in our hands at this moment. And all I did was practice everything I have described up to this point. I believe that my message is an important one. There is value in what I have to say. And on the day that I die, I don't want to have my life flash before my eyes and regret that I never let my positivity create something beautiful in other people. If I published this book at 18, the possibilities really are endless. Not just for me, but for everyone.

Remember my friend:

Every single day has the potential to be the best day of your life. it's up to you. If you are unhappy, the only person that can truly make a difference is you.

Think of your life like a movie. Would you sit through a movie that was sad, boring and predictable? Of course, you wouldn't.

So get out and love everything and everyone around you. Appreciate things for what they are. Take chances, enjoy what you do, and remember that if things get tough, you will always have this letter to turn to. Because it was written to you by someone who cares deeply about you. With the completion of this letter, a small piece of my positivity has now made its way into you.

Do with it what you like.

Make your life the most exciting movie you have ever seen.

Change the world, and know that we are all in this together.

Your friend,

B

Truth

"Never lie to anyone"

He said, as he buttoned up his suit

And got ready for a day at the office.

A day which, contrary to his belief, will be spent lying to no one but himself

Modern Hippy

Adam and Eve

Only got dressed because they were scared

But I am not scared

So I'll spend my days

With my shirt off

Hair blowing in the wind

Not worrying about snakes

Or forbidden fruit

Because nothing that makes you happy

Is ever really forbidden

Trip

The tears won't come

If they know they'll trip on your smile

On the way down

Lemons

Life will give

Lemons.

Don't worry.

Make orange juice from that shit.

Confuse everyone,

Put on one of these:

:)

And enjoy life

Without lemons

Me, Myself, and Me Again, But in My Head

If you talk to yourself, you'll never be lonely

So just go mad

This way,

There will always be a friend

Inside your head

Loop

Always another cigarette to burn

Always another lesson to learn

Always another heart to break

Always more love to make

__Binge__

Perhaps if you stopped looking at the T.V.

And started looking in the mirror

You'd realize that

You are a king

Or a queen

And your powers could be godlike

If only you'd let them

<u>You</u>

You and your records

Your **VINYL**

Are more than just things

Because things are not as addictive

As you and your records

Your **VINYL**

So let's lay together again

Because I'm starting to forget

You and your records

Your **VINYL**

And feeling your skin on my skin

And the music notes on my ears

Will be a quick fix

Quick enough, I think

to satisfy the addiction

Moon

The moon lit up

And in that moment,

her life changed from that of a person

To that of a dream

With the lunar rays

Painting her body

In a new and beautiful way,

making the Earth a canvas

For her new

Breathtaking

Magnificence

F*CK

Tell me:

What's the worst that could happen

If you just finally said

F*ck it

And lived your life the way

You want to live it?

$$ of Speech

Freedom of speech is only

Free

If you don't give a

Damn

About the consequences

Of speaking your mind

Content

Since when did life become a killer?

Since when did people become content

With the very thing that gives them reason to live

Also silently killing them?

20/20 Vision: I can see my dream

I sit here at the computer, alone and with

My glasses off

Like it's a victory of some kind.

Is this what it's like to be a writer?

No, surely it must be lonelier.

After all, I don't fully understand what I write

But I write what I don't fully understand

So I suppose, in some way,

It does seem to come full circle;

Even if I am here with glazed eyes

And an alarm clock that is often much too early

For my liking.

But hey, if you like the words,

It was all worth it, wasn't it?

Yes, I suppose it was

A Letter for Anyone who Needs to Hear it: II

Dear [INSERT NAME HERE]

I believe that all of life can be summed up with one central metaphor/analogy. I like to think of it as the whole "Car and Driver" situation. Let me explain: when a person drives a car, is it the car that's alive or is it the person inside, the operator? Of course I know that you know that it is the operator, and that's what I mean. I think all of human existence is dependent on understanding this concept. Our bodies are simply the cars. Our souls are the operators.

Now, you may be asking yourself what a soul is, "how can I define a soul?" The answer, I think, is not a straightforward one. If it was, nobody would be scared of death or the afterlife. But I think, based on experience, that a person's soul comes from doing the things that make them happy. When someone does something that causes them to laugh out loud or jump for joy, that is the soul. That is the equivalent of rolling down the window of your car and sticking your head out when you are going ten over the limit down the highway. The soul is true freedom. The soul is true, unhinged creativity. The soul is YOU, in your purest form, without any of the stressors of keeping your car in pristine working condition. Let me further the concept of the car and driver by saying this:

If you are driving your car (your real car, not the metaphorical one that actually represents your body) down the highway and the battery dies, does that mean you, as the driver, also die? Of course it doesn't.

That is why I think people needn't be scared of death. I'll admit that it can be a scary concept, but when approached the right way, it can become easier to deal with. The way I see it, death is just your car battery dying. Does that mean the driver dies? Once again, of course not. In fact, for the first time, your soul is free, no longer dependent on your body.

This is why I approach the wall between this physical life and the afterlife as not a wall at all, but a thin barrier that can be conversed. You only need to train your driver to get out of the car temporarily, and you will then be able to sparingly cross the barrier.

I say all this because it is the easiest way to explain some of the experiences I have had. I wouldn't necessarily call them religious, because I know not everyone is religious, and that's okay. But I've definitely experienced some level of spiritual journey, and that, in part, can be attributed to my soul finding a way to manifest itself into the outside world.

All of this is also why I continue to do what I love and enjoy my life. If I can keep my soul in a condition where it feels healthy, I will be able to continually converse with the people who I care about that are no longer driving their cars. These are the people I learn the most from, and I truthfully didn't think it was right to pen a book about love and not acknowledge them.

What I'm meaning to say is, I believe that when a person comes more in touch with their soul, they will find it easier to sense the energy of other souls when they want to be seen or felt.

Even if you are finding this hard to believe, the takeaway is this, I think. Remember what a soul is, and don't lose yours worrying and fretting over things that ultimately aren't going to help make your soul feel more like the purest form of yourself.

Go outside, get dirty, yell at the sky (as loud as you can), and laugh at every stupid joke that you come across.

Because these are the things that are going to make it easier to exit your car when the time comes. If you make it your mission to do everything that makes you happy for the benefit of your soul, you'll come to realize that life is more than just flesh and blood. Life is energy. And if you manifest good energy and surround yourself with people who do the same, your car battery will never really die, will it? :)

First Thought, Best Thought

If you don't believe in god, then you should at least have faith in something.

Whether or not it be god or buddha or the mail main that comes to your door every day, have faith in something. Count on something, please.

People these days simply don't understand that, and it's starting to drive me crazy. It's 2019 and yet we seem to be living in a faithless terrain where people seem to think that if they don't believe in god, they can't believe in anything. This way of thinking has damned our society.

If you don't believe in god, you should perhaps start believing in yourself. This, more than anything, would help the world to become a better place

Because I am not a preacher. What I am is a person who believes that instead of passing blame when something terrible happens, people need to learn to have faith in THEMSELVES. As I've said It is okay to believe in god, or buddha, or whoever you choose to worship. But more than them, you should have faith in yourself. Because whoever or whatever is responsible for putting us on this earth has put us here for a reason. And while I cannot say definitively what that purpose is, I believe the purpose was to create a race that could recognize tragedy and sadness in its species and in its culture to a degree that would move us to do something about it. This is why I say have faith in something, because I believe that this is what we were made to do.

Not plaster the headlines with destruction and sadness.

Instead, work towards helping those people so that their personal tragedies get kept out of the newspapers and online broadcasts. RECOGNIZE THE SUFFERING OF OTHERS AND WORK TO DO SOMETHING ABOUT IT.

I strongly believe that when this kind of faith is demonstrated, simply having faith not necessarily in a god but in our fellow man, that is when the true origin of our faith will be made clear.

That's partially why you hold this book in your hands right now, at this very moment. You were pulled in by the words, and you want to believe that people in this world are capable of love and affection for one another.

THE ONLY PERSON PREVENTING THIS KIND OF BEHAVIOR FROM BECOMING A REALITY IS YOU.

Work to help your fellow man. Make friends with those who struggle until they don't struggle anymore. Use these words to heal your mind, body, and spirit, and when you notice someone else who could use a boost, give this poem to them. I believe that if we all work towards this one common goal of faith and enlightenment for the betterment of our species, the world would become a much more beautiful place.

In the words of John Lennon:

"You may say I'm a dreamer, but I'm not the only one"

After reading this far into the poem, you may be thinking that I should just pack up all the shit that I own and drive away, because "surely a man with ideas this eccentric was not meant to function in the modern world, nor is he ready to."

And certainly, you are entitled to your opinion. But I ask you:

If that is your wish for me, what would be so wrong with that? Maybe that's what the world needs. People with ideas so eccentric, so radical, that they would be willing to put everything on the line, write a book, and drive across the world.

Some of the greatest poets of this generation started a movement that promoted exactly that. Freedom of faith.

Jack Kerouac.

Charles Bukowski.

Allen Ginsberg.

Those men created a generation of people, a MOVEMENT, simply crafted out of their poetry. The world needs more of this. But nowadays, people exercise this faith in a different way. They pierce their faces, get their bodies tattooed, and become modern day hippies, standing for what they believe in.

Not giving a damn what other people think, content with living life just to live it, having faith simply so that they could proclaim that they were faithful.

The world, I think, needs more of this. A new generation of the original hippies and beat poets. Because people talk about the first generation of hippies and beat poets and gypsies as though those people were a type of one off novelty, something that couldn't ever be replaced.

There is a difference between a replacement and an uprising. An uprising of a NEW generation is something that we need.

A new generation of people who, as I said, exercise their passions so furiously they are willing to make their private lives public, their hopes and dreams a reality.

A new generation of people who have faith at least in themselves, and don't rely on a god to fix the wrongs that they have committed.

A new generation of people who, at the end of the day, will put themselves on the line in the name of the creative freedom of those around them.

So please, for the love of Christ, if you don't have faith in God, at least have faith in something. Let's get ourselves out of this slump and realize that if we want life to be worth living, we have to take the steps necessary in order to make that a reality. Something or someone made humans, but now humans make the world. This is our planet. Our time. Our duty to do what needs to done.

So let's do it.

Naked

You could say I'm naked because I sit alone

Sometimes

With no clothes on, completely exposed to anyone who cares to look through the window at me

In my

Natural

Element

You could say I'm naked because I fanaticize

Sometimes

About having a level of intimacy with someone that only comes with removing our clothing and

Loving one anther

Fully and completely, with the lights

On

Or

Off

Or, you could say I'm naked

because

I do not try to hide any ounce of my

Creative being

From anyone who cares enough to ask about it

And as time goes on

You'll realize that

You, too

Are naked.

Just remember, my dear, to only get undressed for the people who will fully understand WHY you are taking off

Your

(physical and mental)

Clothing

You and the Tools

Every tool that we need

To do what we want

Is already in our heads

In our world

You just need

To exercise

Yourself

In a way that

Teaches you how to properly

Use the tools

To build what you need to succeed

Sometimes, I Wonder

Sometimes, I wonder

About everything at once

And then I remember

That it's impossible to wonder about

Everything

Because everything could just as easily

Be defined as absolutely

Nothing

A LETTER TO All Those Who Need to Hear It: III

DEAR [INSERT NAME HERE],

I decided to write this one by HAND because I figure it might have more of A personal effect if you Are Able to Read my handwriting Just As I wrote it.

I often wonder if my writing is easy to understand because Half the time it seems as though I Just scribble things down on to A paper and the words HAPPEN to line up into sentences. I think that's why I like writing so much though. It Reminds me of life. I think people often Just Do things for the sake of Doing them until one Day they wake up and find that their Actions & the choices that they previously thought were ~~the~~ Randomized impulses of the Human Brain were Actually the decisions that contributed to building the life they Are currently living.

see? Just like writing. Words Become sentences (oftentimes subconciously for me, Anyway) And choices Are molded ~~by the~~ the craft the very life we Are All living (Also subconciously, in many cases)

THAT is why I try Not to worry About my writing making perfect sense. Surely the people will make sense of it themselves in a more thorough And concrete way than I ever could. If everything I said made sense, I wouldn't be a writer, I don't think; I wouldn't have anything to wonder about. But there are certain mysteries that I can't seem to solve, so I write about everything I don't understand.

Maybe one day I'll write something worthy of literary scholar.

Maybe one day I'll write something that causes people to better understand why I do what I do.

But for now I think my job is to write so that people understand themselves more than anything else.

I hope this helped.
Your friend,
Bryson

Someday

Someday, I hope that I will live in a house, not too big, but big enough for my family and I, and all the love we will share. And I hope that I won't have to walk in the door after a day at the office and yell:

"I"M HOME"

Because I hope that there will not need to be an office for me to come home from. I only mean that I want my house to be my office, with a plush leather chair in front of a desk made from imported oak, and a computer always sitting, waiting for me to use it to craft my next great message to the world.

And someday, I hope that I am able to look at my wife and my children, and with the most heart-warming sincerity, pass them the book, novella, or magazine that built the house they are standing in.

Someday, I want my wife to be walking down the busy streets of whatever city we are living in, and notice my name in the window of the quaint little local book shop that is owned by a lady named Elanor whose husband built the shop with his bare hands from the ground up.

And I want her to realize that although having my name in Elanor's shop window is nice, I am doing what I do for her sake.

For my beautiful wife, the woman who said yes to my proposal and the woman who raises my children with an insurmountable amount of care and love.

The wife who, although she tries to deny it, is the most beautiful woman I have seen and will ever see.

The wife who I met over coffee at the little suburban coffee shop on eighth street, the one with the plants in the window and the old books of poetry stacked on the magazine rack.

And she will not have lost her beauty since that day, the day when she was wearing a touque that came down over her ears, with her crimson hair flowing like waves down onto her shoulders. The day when she had her feet tucked under the plush chair she was sitting in, perched so beautifully like she was the rightful heir to this long-forgotten coffee shop throne. Even all those years later, she will be the same, if not more beautiful than before.

And someday, I want my children to realize that my unconditional way of life came only from my imagination, with little help from society. Society, I will tell them, tried to convince me otherwise. And if I would have listened, you may not even be here right now.

They of course will be amazed at first, but someday they will understand.

And someday, if an old buddy pops by and says, "How about a round of tequila?"

I want to be able to clap him on the back, kiss my wife on the cheek, and yell:

"This one's on me Jack old boy! Right this way to the finest bar in town!"

And there we will listen to the old crooners play the finest Willie Nelson and Ray Charles covers you'll ever hear, and I'll tip my hat to Jack and say that life is grand, isn't life just grand.

He will reply yes, and we'll go on drinking until the sun goes down and

"Georgia on my Mind" whispers past our ears.

And then Jack will be the one to clap *me* on the back, and he'll say that we probably should be getting home, his wife has been a little off lately.

I'll ask him what he thinks it is, menopause, maybe? And he'll say "Jesus Christ no, she's too young and spry to be getting that at this point." And he will raise his eyebrows at that, as if he thinks that I enjoy the mental picture of him and his wife (Lola, I think her name is) getting intimate in bed together.

But we will go, walking back to my house with our arms around each other, avoiding all the cracks in the sidewalk like we are little kids.

Someday, this someday will be everyday.

Dance

Perhaps

If people danced to words

(Just plain words on a paper)

Like they dance to music,

The world would be better.

Maybe not, but I'd rather try

Then do nothing

At all.

So let's dance, baby

PSA That Never Made the Paper

Attention:

WANTED: someone to drive across the country, with only the clothes on their back and my body beside theirs in the driver's seat.

If you don't know me, and I don't know you,

I'm certain that we both know the sunset.

And I'm equally as certain it will welcome us

into it's

Warm embrace

As we drive into its crimson arms.

My Wedding

I've always said that when the day comes

When I am standing with my wife

Along a big table, that extends

For what seems like miles

And holds all my best friends

Rustyboy

Leslie

Treehouse

Trachsel

My childhood friends, now my groomsmen,

I will refuse to take the time

To individually thank

Each one of the guests for coming.

And it's not because I don't love them.

Actually, quite the opposite.

I love them so much that I want to

Spend the night with them,

Spend MY night with them,

Dancing and laughing and living so

Ferociously that I soak in every moment,

In its beautiful entirety.

And I feel like I wouldn't be able to live

Through the night with this authenticity

If I had to

Stop dancing

Smooth my suit

Put down my drink

And thank relatives.

Because I'd rather overflow with life,

Dance with my wife,

And thank people in advance,

When I stand at the mic.

So that's what this is for,

When the time comes.

THANK YOU, HONESTLY AND SINCERLEY,

FOR COMING. But I just got married

(FLASH RING TO THE CROWD)

And I want to dance.
Not just with her, but with
All of you.

Inspiration Misinformation

For me, inspiration confusing.

Because when I get inspired,

Inspired enough to start writing,

I only wish that I could take this

Inspiration and use it to LIVE

Rather than use it to perch myself

In front of the computer.

And I've just now realized that

Eventually the day will come where

I won't have to make a choice

Between the two.

Because writing in itself will be enough to

Motivate me to LIVE.

The writing will become the inspiration,

Rather than the inspiration becoming

The writing.

Hugs

I can still feel your hugs

And even though the last one

Was

Empty

I don't believe it.

Because last night

You were so very full of life

In such a way that I haven't

Seen in so long.

And so I say I don't believe

Because it's simply impossible

To rid yourself of that zest

In one day and a night.

So give it until morning

And I promise you will feel

Alive

Again.

The sun will come up

And give new life to your hugs

So that

You can open your arms

And not only let me fall in

But also let a little of that

Life

The life worth living,

Leak out.

Okay?

Okay.

Now come here

Dear.

My arms are open,

As they usually are

And as they always will be. You don't need

To worry anymore.

Life leaks out of these pores like sweat

Jazzman

Somehow it all feels so old

Like the jazzman in the bar,

Or the one on Trudy's record player.

Maybe they are the same man.

I can't remember.

In any case, he doesn't take shit from

Nobody, Nowhere.

He only puffs his cigar

Or cigarettes, maybe?

And laughs at the people

Like rats in a race

Always trying to stay ahead.

"You don't need to stay ahead, cat."

He says.

"Everyone is ahead, so long as you ain't

Looking behind. You dig?"

Like a shovel, Jamie. We dig like a

Goddamn shovel

Older

By the time we are all older

And life takes us

And spins us around

Over and over

So that we don't even recognize our

Reflection,

That will be the time when I am most

Alive

And most happy to say

"It's worth living"

And I'll say it every day

So that even if I wake

One morning

And don't remember anything of my life

I'll at least know that

"It's worth living"

Take me back to 2008

The people here

Feel like the stereotypical

Movie characters

From all the old VHS tapes

In the basement.

Cliché jocks and

Mouthy white girls.

And the music is so vividly depicting

The same feeling,

The feeling of the old garage sale,

30 degree

Creamsicle by the pool

Summer days.

Back when Sum 41 and

Blink 182

Played from the old boombox in the garage

While we were all playing with

Action figures in the sandbox.

We were too young to understand the lyrics,

But we didn't have to.

Because now we do, and every time

We hear them,

A tiny part of us gets taken back to

The feeling of the old garage sale,

30 degree

Creamsicle by the pool

Summer days.

And even though I am older, I love that

Feeling,

I will love it always,

And I will never forget that life can

In all it's simplicity, be

Boiled down to

the stereotypical

Movie characters

From all the old VHS tapes

In the basement.

Cliché jocks and

Mouthy white girls.

So let me capture that feeling always,

The feeling of the old garage sale,

30 degree

Creamsicle by the pool

Summer days.

And when I drift off to sleep, I'll wrap

Myself up

And think back to 2008.

Back when things were simple,

And VHS movies were great.

Clean Machine

Sometimes, I think

You need to clean your room

Not to simply clean it,

But perhaps for a bigger purpose.

Clean it

So that when you wake up

You feel like a different

Person

In a different house

Ready to wake up

And live a new life.

Maybe that's all you need

Thrift Dreams

I bought a sweater for three

Dollars

And some corduroys for

Seven.

A ball cap for

Five.

And with the rest of my money

I bought a mickey of rum

And some cheap dollar store Cola.

The red solo cups were free,

I found them in the cupboard.

My clothes aren't Gucci

But I FEEL rich,

And that's the important part,

I think.

I may be living in a thrift dream,

But at least I'm drinking

A man's drink.

Cheers.

History

I wrote this in history class

Because

I hope someday it will go down in

History

And instead of studying

The overpopulation of fish in the

1800s

Children will instead be studying

The joys of life

And how to live it

Lakes

Let's start swimming in lakes of water

Again, instead of lakes of money.

Because no fish can swim in money,

And neither can we, if it gets deep

Enough

Can I

Can I watch movies with you

Instead of staying upstairs alone?

Can I turn my music up

Loud enough to wake the

Neighbors?

Can I scream at the sky

Until my vocal chords rip

And I am left as a mute for the rest

Of my life?

Can I talk to myself in my head

Long enough to make myself Go mad?

Can I unlock the door to my house

And lay on the kitchen floor

Just because I am tired

And need to rest?

Of course I can.

Because if this proves anything,

It's that I can do anything I want,

Whenever I want,

For the rest of my days
Until I die.
And I'll make sure I remember that
Because I never want to grow up
To a point where I lose my free will.
Because in between graduation
And "real life"
There is a small space,
And in that space there is a place for
the
Misfits
Losers
Dreamers
Entrepreneurs
And peacekeepers.
And I know that if I can stay in that
Space, I can live there forever,
And "Can I?"
Will not be a question.
Because I CAN, and I won't even have
To ask.
I'll just know.

AFTERWORD

And just like that, you've reached the end. Much like the introduction, I've thought a lot about how I want to end this book. It's a lot longer than I thought it was going to be, but I think that's okay. I for one, don't mind, and I hope you didn't either. That last poem, "Can I?" embodies everything I feel, I think. If you haven't gotten a proper taste of how I view things before you got to that poem, I think you could read that one all by itself and get a good idea of who I am.

When I first started this book, I knew I wanted to make something positive, so that if people were ever feeling not positive, I could give them something to turn to. I've accomplished my goal (in my eyes, anyway) and I hope you can use this book as a sort of guide for life. Because my wish for everyone who has read up to this point is this:

Be the person I've written about in these poems. The person who simply doesn't care what other people think, and lives life because they love it. Because really, there's nothing more to life, in my mind. I believe we were put here to simply enjoy our time, and nothing else. So please, don't worry my friends. Everything will be okay, I promise. This book is proof of that.

And y'know, if you're sad that you've reached the end, don't be. Because as fun as writing this book has been, I'm sort of glad it's done. And not because I didn't love writing it. I love this book more than anything. But I say I'm happy because now I'll be able to wake up every morning, and before I go to the bathroom or get my coffee, I'll be able to glance at a copy of this book on my nighstand and know that what I've created will be on the earth forever. Because it won't just be a document on the computer anymore. By the time I see it on my nighstand, it will be an actual tangible collection of my thoughts. And that's why I'm happy it's done. Because now other people will be able to enjoy what I've made. They'll be able to kick back after a hard day at work, and use MY work to unwind.

Another thing I want to make note of is the fact that I have never actually finished a book until now. I've always had ideas, and I've always started, but I've never been able to stay motivated enough to finish. That's why I think this collection is special. Because this is the one I did finish. That's how much this means to me, and that's how much I want it to mean to you, to all of you. The book that you are holding is the first one that kept me motivated enough to write nearly 100 poems. And I think that's interesting, because I've never written poetry before. In fact, up until the start of this year, I wasn't even really interested in poetry. Like I said in the introduction, everything I have written prior to this has been fiction. And while I do still enjoy writing those stories, the completion of this book has taught me that I don't need to make up fake new worlds in order to keep myself interested. Through poetry, I've been able to find the beauty in the natural world, the one right in front of us. This is the world I want to continue to explore.

I suppose what I'm trying to say is that I know I'll be back with another project, but I don't know when. I need time to think and unwind. I'm approaching an extremely exciting and interesting new chapter in my life, and I intend to go into it with an open mind. A mind that isn't concerned with what to write and when to write it, but instead with an undesirable appreciation for everything around me.

But until I get back, remember to love one another, hold each other close, appreciate the little things, and never let yourself slip away. Be who you want to be, rather than a projection of what you think would appeal to others.

Also, I have to say, don't try to analyze my poems to a degree where you lose sight of what they are actually about. They simply weren't meant to be analyzed. They were meant to be enjoyed as they were written, with little hidden meaning behind them. These are just thoughts on a page, after all.

Anyway, thank you. Thank you for purchasing this art and reading this far, and internalizing everything I have written. Thank you for expanding your horizons and opening yourself up to these radical ideas. I promise you that because of this, your life will change. There was a reason you picked up this book, and now that you've finished, you can begin to manifest the positive energy from these pages into your own life. I think that everything happens for a reason. I wrote this book for a reason, much like you read this book for a reason. Even if it was subconscious desire, I know that when you cracked the spine on this book and began to read, you were looking for something.

I hope you found it. I know I did.

I love you all.

Bryson Tyrick Bolianatz

♡

About the Author

Bryson Tyrick Bolianatz is a musician, writer, artist, and life enthusiast. He grew up on an acreage outside of Pilot Butte, Saskatchewan, and will soon reside in Saskatoon Saskatchewan, where he plans to further his writing career.

After being denied publication by various literary magazines, he decided to write and self-publish his debut poetry collection.

L.O.V.E. is a result of his efforts. It is his first collection.

Contact:

Brysontyrick18@gmail.com

@writingofbtbolianatz